Within the Soul of a Woman

A poetry book of life, love, betrayal, and loss

ANIKA B. ADDERLY

Within the Soul of a Woman

Copyright © 2022 by Anika B. Adderly, in Association with Emerging Woman Publishing

All rights reserved.

No portion of this book may be reproduced, stored in a retrieval system, or transmitted in any form by any means – electronic, mechanical, photocopy, recording, or other – except for brief quotations in printed reviews, without prior permission of the author.

Second Edition

Printed in the United States of America

ISBN-979-8-9866102-0-7

ISBN-979-8-9866102-1-4

Dedication

For My Loving Aunt Helen, My Vibrant Velvet Rose,
My Cheerleader, My Confidant, My Friend

I Love you!!

Acknowledgements

First, I would like to acknowledge my Lord and Savior Jesus Christ, because without him I am nothing. I thank him for his Love, Grace, and Mercy.

To my family, and friends thank you for continuing to pour into me, so that God can pour out!

Contents

*Commit your activities to the Lord, and your plans
will be established.*

Proverbs 16:3 (CSB)

Letter to the Soul of a Woman

Dear Courageous Woman,

I may not know your story, but I know that we share a special bond. The trials of being a woman is sometimes second to none, but always remember God knows our strengths and weakness too, and our Father is the only one in this life who can carry us through. It is within these pages that I share with you the gift that my Father has given me. Each poem represents a certain area in my life rather it's my pain, my struggles, my family, or life itself; Because I've come to realize in this life were never by ourselves. It is my prayer that we learn to be kind to one another, accept our faults, love ourselves, and forgive ourselves just as Jesus Christ has forgiven us. Remember each one of us are unique in your own special way, and God's plan for us always outweigh our own.

So, no matter what direction life has taken you; Always remember… It is Our Strength, Our Bravery, Our Perseverance, Our Assurance, Our Love, Our Hope, Our Prayers, and Our Faith that will always carry us through….

Blessings always,

Anika

A man's heart plans his way, But the LORD directs his steps.

Proverbs 16:9 (NJKV)

Sis! If God is for you, then who can be against you?

(Author Paraphrased)

Encourage yourself, Love yourself, Forgive yourself, Believe in yourself!

And Keep Going!

Within the Soul of a Woman

Betrayal

The Death of a Marriage

Time to Move On

Eleven years of laughter, smiles, tears, and craziness too.

Eleven years of plans and commitments too always stay true.

Eleven years we've prayed together, stayed together, and yes also laid together,

But the best gift of all was our beautiful son we made together.

We said we could make it through the storms and the rain, but when the storms came, you felt ashamed.

The day we became one was always a dream come true,

Many said we wouldn't make it, but I believed and trusted in you.

But then the gossip, enemies, and harlots came you refused to stand on marriage and its sacred name.

For you were taken by the streets, the lust, and blindness of another,

You forgot all about your son and his mother,

You continued to spread your lies, and never admitted to

your own faults, but that's okay, God got me and our son, and we're never alone.

So, my dear, choose the streets, the games, and the lies they tell, but believe me when I say, "It is well; It is well."

Times are hard, and the struggle is real.

Real for you to know, indeed, Life Lessons are for real!

There was always an alignment for three an alignment from God to you, then me,

but now the alignment has been broken and the vows you promised are gone.

I wish you well, my love, but heaven and I know it's

time to move on.

Excerpt from:

When To: Walk, Wait & Pray

© 04/ 2019 Anika B. Adderly

Poet / Author

Gratitude

Through it all I trust you

What Will This Day Bring?

As I start my day on my knees in prayer sometimes, I ask myself God are you really there? I study your word and meditate too, but sometimes this life becomes so hard that I don't know what to do.

I cry out because I know your real, but there are times that I have to express how I feel.

The bills keep coming month after month, and nothing seems to change: The lack of funds, and the lack of food, and there are times it feels like my health is failing too, but through it all I have to trust your word, because there's no one else to turn too.

Through all my mistakes, choices, and tears too; I thank you Lord because you have always pulled me through.

What will this day bring? I honestly don't know. I do know that you will never leave me, nor forsake me, and you're with me wherever I go.

What will this day bring? I guess I will have to wait and see, because it's you who knows all, and sees all; It's you who directs my destiny.

@ 07/2016

The Blessing

The sounds of the birds chirping on my windowpane is so majestic during the early morning rain. As, I look out my window into the trees, I have to give thanks for what I see.

I see the sun shining high in the sky, I see the birds flying ever so high, I see the trees blowing in the wind, I see that God has bless me to start a new day all over again.

Today, is not promise as I already know, but I have to give you praise before I walk out this door.

Holy Spirit have thy own way, and please always abide; Continue to comfort and lead me, reassure me that you're always by my side. Heavenly Father, I ask that you bless my son, and please bless me; My prayer today is that you bless and protect my entire family; Bless my friends, and foes too because they have no idea that all my blessings flow from you.

Dear Father, I ask that you bless our elders, widows, and the children too, feed the hungry, and heal the sick. Father God protect and direct those souls that's lost in the streets; Help me to show compassion and be kind to everyone I meet.

I pray a special blessing that you cover, and protect us all, because Lord if you don't, we will surely fall.

@ 11/2020

Perceptive

My Beautiful Daughter

My Dearest Lilia

My dearest Lilia the time has come that God has called your name and welcomed you home. No final exchange of words was spoken neither a goodbye amongst us too; for you were gone within a twinkling of an eye as a piece of me died along with you.

I will forever cherish the times we had, and the moments we shared; The good the bad, the happy, and the sad. For I am forever thankful for this time that the Father has trusted and blessed me with you. I've experienced your kindness, your love, your beauty, your creativeness, your wittiness, your smiles, and your cries. I've experienced that undying love that a mother has for her child.

Now the tears will flow, and my heart will ache too, for God is the only one who truly knows how much I really love you. We will think about you always for you will never be forgotten, you are a part of lives forever my precious dear Lilia.

It breaks my heart to lose you, but you did not go alone. A part of me went with you the moment God called you home.

My beautiful daughter although I can no longer see you, nor share in our intimate talks; I will feel your presence all around me, rather it comes by sunlight, or rain the blowing of the wind, or the sweet singing of the birds our lives have forever been changed.

I will not say goodbye now for we will meet again. My dearest Lilia that I once cradled in my arms, and nursed upon my breast the time has come for you to take your heavenly rest.

@ 06/2021

My Velvet Rose

A Queen of Hearts

A Rose for the Queen

A vibrant velvet rose that's fit for a Queen. A Queen of substance, generosity, integrity, and compassion, this rose has embarked upon on her final chapter. A rose that represents love, life, joy, and laughter. This rose is well defined by her personality as well as her character.

My velvet rose grew for all to see, this rose loves both you and me. We will carry this rose forever in our hearts, because we know that Ammie Jones played an important part.

May God wipe the tears we sow because she's at home and this I know!

A place like no other where the walls are of jasper, and the streets are paved with gold. This is a place where we should strive to be; this is the place that Jesus Christ waits for you and for me.

She's at peace and gone on to rest for we all know that Ammie gave her very best. The Father awaits her, and her Mother too what more could you ask God to do?

Don't you cry, nor shed a tear for I am always with you my precious dear.

I laughed, I danced, I smiled, and I prayed: I cooked, I cleaned, I traveled, and I loved to sing. I've lived my life to the fullest my beloved.

So, burn your candle, and watch the flame look closely as you whisper my name. For I am always with you watching you as you sleep; Please know that I am fine; I'm resting at my Savior's feet.

So, take care of each other, and I love you all, but the time has come that I had to answer my Father's call.

@ 02/11/2022

Teachings of Life

Lay the Foundation

Darling Black Girl

My darling black girl, come sit beside me in this chair and let your momma comb your thick coarse hair. I want to talk to you, and I need you to be quiet and listen.

I need you to know that you are an African Princess with a heart of gold, and this world is at your feet, so make sure to take hold.

There are some people in this world that might be threaten by your intellect, your beauty, your ingenuity, your smile, your grace, your education, your knowledge as well as your race, but never allow anyone to degrade you because the color of your skin always remember that true beauty lies deeply within.

For you are the beauty of your Father's eye and this my love I cannot deny.

Learn to embrace your melanin flawless skin, your round nose, and full cherry lips as well as your curvaceous big hips.

Our race is strong, beautiful, vigorous, creative, and courageous too. The strength, the spirits, and cries of our ancestors' flow throughout your veins; Its' their hopes and dreams that have been laid out for you, so my darling girl its' up to you to make sure all your dreams come true.

Never allow anyone to crush your spirit, nor give grief to your soul always know that your life is more precious than silver or gold.

Stand strong in your truth, your vision, and your dreams until they unfold.

Know who you are and understand what that means; you are more than a pretty face, with a small waist, and a big butt there is so much more to you than what's between your thighs.

The world will be so much better if they took the time to recognize the knowledge, the power, the tenacity, and your talent inside.

Always hold your head up high with your back straight and look people directly in the eye; Let them know you are royalty, and a woman of faith as you pass them by.

My darling girl listen to my words as momma tell you the truth, learn to know your worth, protect your peace, protect your power, protect your home, and your babies too.

Learn when to stay and walk away from things and people who could lead you astray.

Learn how to love and forgive because this my love is the secret to how we all should live.

Take your place in this world, and never bow down in defeat. Choose your words and your battles; learn when to hold your tongue and learn when to speak.

My beautiful darling girl I hope you understand, and listen to what I'm saying to you, because this world can be cruel and unkind, but if you listen and follow momma words you will be just fine.

@ 05/2020

Choose Wisely Son

You're my first born and only son I leave you the inheritance that was passed down to me; I leave you strength, courage, knowledge, wisdom, and discerning intellect.

May the strength of Samson, the heart of David, the wisdom of Solomon, the courage of Daniel, and the love of Christ reside in the depth of your soul.

Oh, how I reminisce on those days when I would snuggle you to keep you warm, hold your hands, or sing you to sleep; Those are the days that I asked the Lord to watch over you as you sleep.

I remember the first day when I walked you to class, you let go of my hand and said "Mommy, I'm a big boy now." And I knew that my tears will soon pass.

When you were just an infant people would stop and plant seeds in your life, so many times I heard them say "There is a special calling on your son's life."

Son, no matter how difficult the road in the future may

seem to be, always remember the seeds are planted, and this you must believe.

The day will come when you feel angry, frustrated, and doubt will start to heed those are the times I need you to remember that Jesus died to set you free.

Never allow violence, peer pressure, temptation, nor greed to disrupt your path. You're a man of integrity, faith, intelligence, compassion, respect, and character these are the qualities of a good man and son they all matter.

Your faith will be tested but stand your ground anyway; Put on the whole amour of God and you know how to pray.

When the enemy comes, and it feels as though you're under attack; Remember that the angels will descend from heaven and the greatest Warrior of all has your back.

My son you will meet many people and different women in this life, so please be careful when you choose who should become your wife. Do not choose her from your flesh, or with a lustful eye this woman should be honest with a keen virtue, and you know the reason why. She is sharp, honest, beautiful, knowledgeable, caring, and smart this woman will make sure you do your part.

She will love you, respect you, and hold you accountable. She will pray with you and for you before she goes to sleep, she will have a kindred spirit and kind heart make sure you love her, protect her, and cover her spiritually, physically, and emotionally.

She will build with you and trust you to keep her, and your family safe; Make sure you treasure and adore her because she will be worth the wait.

This type of woman you will never meet hanging in the streets and doing nothing in life because she understands the importance of building and establishing herself in this tedious life.

This woman will walk with you hand and hand and have a personal relationship with Jesus Christ this is the woman someday that will make you a beautiful wife.

@ 12/2019

Strength and Wisdom

Trust in the Lord with all your heart and lean not on your own understanding; in all your ways acknowledge him and he shall direct thy paths.

Proverbs 3:5-6 (KJV)

Grandmother's Prayer

I taught my family how to love, I taught my family how to forgive, I taught my family to be kind, and I taught my family how to live, but most importantly I taught my family how to pray, and trust in God along the way.

When you get tired, and your body aches with pain remember that there is power in Jesus Holy Name.

When the world is cruel, and you don't know what to do, call his name because his love will never change.

I've prayed for you, I've cried for you, and I've fasted for you too. I've given you my best, I've passed my test, now it's up to God to handle the rest.

Remember your strength comes from God, your family, and your roots too, but know there's nothing in this life that automatically belongs to you.

It all belongs to God for his word is true, he created us in his imaged when he breathed life into you.

He's your Savior, your Healer, your Strength, your Protector, your Provider, and your Guide; Always remember he walks alone your side.

He gives Grace, and Mercy that's not rightfully yours, so never become so consumed to believe that this world is actually yours.

Your Grandmother prayed and cried many tears asking God to never leave your side, I've kept this prayer in my heart unto the very day that I died.

Our happy times and happy tears remember to hold onto them throughout the years.

Teach the children what's right and wrong; Teach the children that they shall never walk alone; Teach the children that they should pray; And Teach the children that Jesus Christ is the only way!

I'm forever thankful and blessed for the years that I've shared with you. I thank God for All My Children! My Grands, Great Grands, and Great – Great Grands too; Always remember that Grandma Susie B. truly loves you!

To all my children!! Remember my words, keep God close to your heart, and let him lead the way, because it is my hope, and prayer that I will see all my family on that Glorious Beautiful Day!

@ 05/2018

A Mother's Plea

The Sins of a Son

A Mother's Prayer

Someone asked me why do I feel so compelled to write about my fallen black brother? I had to ask them have you ever sat down and talk to one's mother.

I remember hearing the trembling in her voice, and ooh the thinness of her frame; It's a wonder why this woman has not gone insane?

Take a look around! And see what's going on. See the pain in a mother's eyes as she asks herself "Lord is this my child?" I didn't raise him like this, and God knows I did the best I can, but when his father walked out on us, my little boy felt that he had to become a man.

Now he's in the streets wasting his life away my knees become so tired that all I can do is pray.

I pray for strength, and I pray for guidance, I pray for that little light to come on inside of him; There's got to be a better way! You don't have to kill and steal. I've always pictured you as the immaculate young man, the strong father, and devoted husband now I see you as a threat to yourself and taking the life of another.

Am I, his keeper? Is this my fault? Am I responsible for the shootings he's committed, the dropping out of school? A mother should never utter the words "My boy is a damn fool!" Or better yet should I close my ears, and shut my eyes and toss this issue aside?

Everywhere I go I see a young black brother's picture plastered on a billboard wanted for murder, or robbery so many things Lord, and sometimes even sodomy.

I look at their faces, and my heart races with fear. Lord help him! Bring my child closer near; Nearer to thee, and nearer to you I give you all the praise what more could a mother do?

Instead of using the words bitches, and whores and yes even Nigga! Replace this language and educate yourselves learn about your American Literature.

Learn your history and know from where you came. Learn about the struggles and trials that your ancestor's life was not all in vain.

Learn what they went through and feel their pain. Imagine the whips the lashes and Ohh! Yes, definitely the chains.

My beautiful black son where have you gone? I clinched my heart with hope, and fear while I recite this song.

A song that I sang when you were just an infant, a song so precious and ever so true, a song of unconditional love in all that life takes us through. A song of my beautiful black baby boy that I pledged my eternal life too, but now that your grown and out on your own; Life has turned into nothing but a bitter agonizing and troubling song.

@ 08/2010

Resilience

Beauty for Ashes

I AM ME

I am unique, and creative some say I am tenacious and sometimes crazy.

I am a mother, a friend, a veteran, a student, an author, an entrepreneur, a child of God, the Daughter of a King, yet I've been called everything in between.

I cry, I scream, and sometimes I've been very mean.

I am beautiful, I am strong, I am intelligent, I am worthy, I am a vibrant young Queen.

I have scars from the war, and wounds unseen these are blemishes from my past beyond from what one could ever see.

I've been tossed and driven battered by an angry sea.

I was left and broken of an unanswered why? My tears soaked my sheets as I asked the Lord "Why Oh Why?" But how faithful is he for now I see that the answer truly laid inside of me.

For he took me up and laid me in his arms he reminded me child that I've already won.

I am someone's hero, someone's answered prayer, I am a rare diamond in the rough, who have had her share of more than enough.

I am courageous and fearless, yet sometimes gentle and sweet, for it is I who can always come kneel before my Savior's feet.

For I am someone special in my own little way, and that's more than enough for what my enemies have to say.

Now, faith is the substance of the things hoped for, and the evidence of these unseen, yet never will I forget or allow you to forget that you are a child of a Mighty King.

@ 09/2020

Look to the Hills

I will look to the hills from where my help comes from; All of my help comes from the Most High who sits on his throne in the Heavenly sky.

He's the Creator of the world, He's the Great I Am, He's what you need him to be; He's far beyond from what you and I could ever see.

I will look to the hills when I feel tired and lost; It's in the hills that I remember my life came with a cost.

It's in the hills where I will find comfort, grace, mercy, and reassurance to pass this difficult race. It's in the hills where my body, my mind, and my spirit can lay down and rest.

It's in the hills where my God does his very best.

It's in the hills where my soul finds peace, quietness, tranquility, deliverance, and restoration,

It's in the hills where he will wrap, and clothed me with strength and dignity, He will love on me, and lead me safety through, my God will do exactly what I need him too.

It's in the hills where he crafts the masterpiece, and mold me in his hands, it's here where he will give me the ability to understand that my life is safe in the palm of his hands.

@ 03/2017

Clarity

A Three Strand Cord

Do you see me?

Do you see me when you hold my hand? Do you see the woman who is not afraid to stand? Do you see my worries, my fears, and the wrinkles throughout the years? Do you see the parts of me when I am serious and playful too? You have to see me before I say the words "I Do."

I've lived the lies, I've said the goodbyes, and I've had the heartaches too, I've forgiven myself and I've learned to love myself, that's what a strong woman has got to do.

So, make sure you understand that I am not a woman who will go chase after a man.

I've raised my son, I've stood on my own, and I've gone back to school too, so before this thing goes any further, I need you to see that I am becoming the woman who God created me to be.

I might not be a size six, nor a size eight, but these gifts that I carry are so much greater than my weight.

I carry the gifts of love, honesty, discernment, and devotion too; I carry the gifts of companionship, friendship, and understanding, but most importantly I carry the gifts of a praying woman, a praying mother, and a praying wife too, but you need to understand that this relationship has got to be a part of God's plan.

I want to take long walks on the beach with our toes buried in the sand; I want you to push me on the swing and have a picnic in the dark; I want us to cuddle, laugh and sing with each other long after its' dark; I want us to worship together, pray together, and fast together too; I want us to raise our families, and love one another just as Jesus Christ told us too.

So, before you give me this ring, and ask me to be your wife. Please understand this ring doesn't mean a thing unless were committed in life.

@ 02/2021

Inner Strength

Know who you are, and to thyself be true; believe in yourself, and your calling the way God intended for you. The beauty of your calling lies within your soul, there are times that we have to uncover what's buried so deep until it unfolds. The inner strength of a woman is a beautiful thing to see: It's her strength, her dignity and her wisdom that's held to a higher degree.

It's through her hardships, humiliations, and trials too; it's her cries, her tears, her burdens that she has carried throughout the years; Her life experiences, and all she's gone through is just a small testament for God is getting ready to do.

When adversity choose to come your way hold your head up high, because you know that a strong woman must pray.

Don't engage in lies, and foolishness with the tip of your tongue, because girl! You know your best days are yet to come.

I'm a woman of strength, and I love who I see, I will no longer allow anyone in my space who chooses to disrespect me. I'm a woman of strength, I will emerge, and be free, I will always remember my Savior who was crucified and died just for me.

His love, and his blood is something to behold, he's given me the strength, and the power to make sure my story is told. So, I will continue to walk, and share the good news, I will continue to do exactly what he told me too.

I will continue to love and honor this beautiful black woman who God created me to be, I will continue to nurture and respect this black woman whom he has set free.

@ 03/2022

I Thank you

Happy Days, Happy Days it's time to stand up and cheer. I thank you Lord that my days have all become so very clear.

The doors of opportunities are starting to line up now, and I can see the purpose of my calling. I see the emptiness that you had to fill; I see it clearly now that I wasn't completely healed.

Every lesson, every trial, every loss, and every tear was just building me for a particular skill.

Father you are the potter, and I am the clay I thank you Lord for leading, protecting and guiding me along the narrow way.

@ 06/2022

Fear not, for I am with you; Be not dismayed, for I am your God. I will strengthen you, Yes, I will help you, I will uphold you with My righteous right hand.

Isaiah 41:10 (NKJV)

Closing Notes from the Author

I want to thank each one of you for your love, and support. Although, this poetry book is quite short its' also quite impactful, and very sentimental. I'm sure that some of you can relate to at least one poem that was written. Honestly, I never thought about consolidating my poems into a book because I wanted to wait until I had written more. However, it wasn't until my Aunt's Homegoing Celebration that I recited a poem she asked me to write; After receiving many compliments about my work, and how touching the words were I decided to consolidate what I had written over the years and put it in an e-book. Now, that I think about it this book was birthed while mourning a loved one. Isn't it just like God to show up at our weakest and most vulnerable moment?

I share all of this with you to let you know there is never a perfect, nor exact time to pursue what God has placed in your heart to do. Remember OUR

Father can bring Happiness, and Joy from our Tears and Sorrow!

Continue to go after your dreams, be bold, be intentional, and be great!

Love to you all,

Anika

Your Personal Thoughts

Your Personal Thoughts

Were you able to relate to a poem? If so, how?

How do you Express your Inner Feelings / Emotions?

What are some ways you heal
from your pain?

Forgiveness doesn't always come easy; How do you deal with forgiving yourself and others?

Coming this Fall

12/2022

It is the pressures, frustrations, and trials of life that can make the strongest individual feel tired, defeated, and helpless, but through prayer, meditations, applying the word of God and trusting him all things are possible.

In this 21 Day Prayer Journal Anika takes you on the emotional roller coasters of life that every woman has endured rather its' feeling inadequate, lost, betrayed, depressed, forgotten, unloved, or frighten.

Please turn the page for a preview of

My 21 Day Prayer Journal

*Learning to Love yourself, through the Painful,
and Emotional Journeys of Life*

Prologue

In this Prayer Journal I have created 21 lessons; Before you begin your day, I ask that you set aside at least 10 minutes to pray and meditate. Believe it or not prayer prepares you for the challenges that you will encounter throughout the day, and throughout your life; Honestly, what better way to acknowledge and thank our Heavenly Father and Lord and Savior Jesus Christ but through Prayer, Worship and giving Praise. Whatever strategy you use to surround yourself with his presence do it! As for me when I was going through my valley experience, I would use sticky notes to post scriptures, quotes, declarations, and affirmations all around me: To include my bathroom mirror, my bedroom, and my kitchen; Still to this day in whatever situation I find myself in I pray, read and post sticky notes pertaining to that matter all around me. I am determined to surround my-self with God's word and his promises pertaining to my life. In this journal you will see that I have included several teaching tools to help you along your 21- day journey. Also, some personal stories, and struggles of my own. It is my hope and prayer that enjoy reading My 21 Day Prayer Journal.

DAY 1 Declaration

Lord God, I thank you for blessing me to see another day. I thank you for loving me in spite of me loving myself. I thank you because you are my Father, my healer, my confidant, my protector, my shield, and my all. I choose this day to live my life always trusting you, depending on you now, and forever more.

LESSON ONE!

Give Thanks – Give thanks unto the LORD, for he is good; his love endures forever (Psalm 107:1 NIV).

The first thing I do in the morning is give thanks to our Heavenly Father. I absolutely love waking up to the sounds of birds chirping or singing early in the morning. If the animals can give praise to our Heavenly Father, then so should we. Before you begin your day, I ask that you set aside 10-15 minutes to read and meditate on the word of God. This way you are preparing your mind and spirit to face whatever challenges that may come your way.

Listed below is your first exercise as you begin your 21-day journey; Please remember to be honest and transparent in answering all the questions that's being ask of you. Afterall, were in this together to better ourselves in the long run for the Kingdom and for his Glory.

1. What am I thankful for?

____

____

____

____

____

____

____

2. How much time am I willing to read and study God's word on a daily basis?

____

____

____

____

____

____

3. Why is it so important to acknowledge the goodness of God over my life?

____

____

____

____

____

4. What Am I expecting God to do in my life?

____

____

____

____

____

Scripture to Read, Study and Learn

- *Rejoice always, pray continually, give thanks in all circumstances; for this is God's will for you in Christ Jesus* (1 Thessalonians 5:16-18 NIV).

- *Let the peace of Christ rule in your hearts, since as members of one body you were called to peace. And be thankful* (Colossians 3:15 NIV).

Day 2 Declaration

Today is the day that I choose to remember "Who I Am and Whose I Am." I know my Father will continue to shield me and protect me as he did for Daniel in the Lion's Den and the 3 Hebrew boys (Shadrach, Meshach, and Abednego) in the Fiery Furnace. No matter what situation comes my way, I know that I am never alone.

LESSON TWO!

WHO ARE YOU? – I am the vine; you are the branches. He who abides in Me, and I in him, bears much fruit; for without Me you can do nothing (John 15:5 CSB).

Personal Note

Living and growing in Christ involves building and maintaining a personal and intimate relationship with him on a daily basis.

1. Have you built a personal relationship with Jesus Christ? If not, what's stopping you?

____

____

____

____

2. Take a moment to define yourself through your own eyes.

____

____

____

____

3. Are you happy with whom you, see?

____

____

____

____

4. Now define yourself through the eyes of your Father. Who does God say you are?

____

____

____

____

____

5. Whose vision will you choose, and why?

____

____

____

____

____

6. Why is it important to establish a strong and intimate relationship with Jesus Christ?

____

____

____

____

____

There are times that we become so accustomed to the labels that others placed on us; Rather it's being a mother, wife, sister, girlfriend, co-worker, or a friend. Don't you know that there's so much more to you? Do not get comfortable living your life stagnant; there's something great inside of you. Hold your head up high, put a smile on your face, sip your tea, know your worth, and pursue your dreams; Remember who lives within you.

Scripture to Read, Study and Learn

- *Therefore, if anyone is in Christ, he is a new creation; old things have passed away; behold, all things have become new* (2 Corinthians 5:17 NKJV).

- *But you are a chosen generation, a royal priesthood, a holy nation; His own special people, that you may proclaim the praises of Him who called you out of darkness into His marvelous light* (1 Peter 2:9 NKJV).

DAY 3 Declaration

Today, I take full responsibility for my own actions, I will no longer hide my tears, my guilt, my shame, nor my embarrassing moments. If I must cry then I will cry, but I will keep going. My future is looking ever so bright. What's behind me is in the past, but what's before me is the winning goal.

LESSON THREE!

Learning the Lesson - Don't worry I am with you.

Don't be afraid I am your God. (Isiah 41:10 ERV).

1. What past life experiences are keeping you
   hostage?

   ____

   ____

   ____

2. What are some valuable and teachable lessons
   that you have learned from your past?

   ____

   ____

   ____

3. What extra weight do you need to remove from
   your life so that God can take you higher?

   ____

   ____

   ____

4. Are you living to please others? If so, why?

   ____

   ____

   ____

5. **What steps will you implement today that will enable you to become a better you?**

____

____

____

Doesn't it feel good to be at a position in life where you feel comfortable, love, and secure? But that feeling can easily change when you find yourself stuck and afraid. You know that place in life where you feel everyone is judging you, or better yet you're judging yourself. It's that place in one's life where you might feel agitated, empty, loss, or stagnant. We've all cross that path at one time or the other, but the goal is to become unstuck, and move in the direction of endless possibilities.

In the next exercise I want you to write out a prayer asking the Holy Spirit to free you from any bondage, troublesome life experiences, or any negative thoughts; Whatever it may be that has prevented you from moving forward in life.

Personal Note

"Remember in order to receive you must let go of the guilt, the anger, and the fear that has kept you hostage."

To learn more about Anika B. Adderly or check for new upcoming books, log onto our website:

www.anikaadderly.com

www.ingramcontent.com/pod-product-compliance
Lightning Source LLC
Chambersburg PA
CBHW040104150726
48005CB00013B/1570